THE ZERO-WASTE KITCHEN

DELICIOUS RECIPES AND SIMPLE IDEAS TO HELP YOU REDUCE FOOD WASTE

CHARMAINE YABSLEY

summersdale

THE ZERO-WASTE KITCHEN

An Hachette UK Company
www.hachette.co.uk

Summersdale Publishers Ltd
Part of Octopus Publishing Group Limited
Carmelite House
50 Victoria Embankment
LONDON
EC4Y 0DZ
UK

www.summersdale.com

Printed and bound in China

ISBN: 978-1-78783-690-7

Substantial discounts on bulk quantities of Summersdale books are available to corporations, professional associations and other organizations. For details contact general enquiries: telephone: +44 (0) 1243 771107 or email: enquiries@summersdale.com.

CONTENTS

Introduction

If you knew that you were throwing away a substantial sum of money every year, you'd probably take a long hard look at your spending habits. Yet, in America, approximately one meal (1,217 calories) of food goes in the bin per person every day, and the UK wastes 6.6 million tonnes every year – enough to fill the Royal Albert Hall 96 times!

And all this wasted food adds up. Not just in your bin, but in landfills in the ground and emissions in the air. Food that is lost or wasted costs the global economy close to £470 billion each year. If you add up the annual waste from every household around the world, it's a shocking 1.3 billion tonnes of food, enough to fill 234,000 Olympic-sized swimming pools.

The Western world is responsible for discarding the most food. Research shows that USA, Canada, Australia and New Zealand waste:

- **52 per cent of fruit and vegetables**
- **50 per cent of seafood**
- **38 per cent of grain products**
- **22 per cent of meat products**
- **20 per cent of milk**

In sub-Saharan Africa, South and South-East Asia, by comparison, the average person only throws away 6 to 11 kg of food waste a year.

Even though it might seem we have surplus food, almost 11 per cent of people around the world go hungry. It's believed that if even just one quarter of the food that is currently being wasted was saved, it would be enough to feed 870 million people.

Around 8 per cent of greenhouse gases is caused by food waste.

In reducing your food waste, you'll be helping to cut greenhouse gas emissions and water wastage. And as our world population grows, this change in thinking is more important than ever. It's estimated that by 2050 the world's population will be around nine billion people. If we continue to waste food at the same rate, yet still want to ensure everybody has enough to eat, we'll need to produce 70 per cent more food than we do today. By learning how to eliminate food waste

and use food scraps, leftovers and almost out-of-date foods in a positive, proactive way, the strain on the environment will be much less.

Over time, we have lost the knowledge involved in food preparation and cooking. We peel fruits and vegetables, discarding the skin, roots, stems and leaves which are edible and can be used. Many fruits and vegetables contain the majority of nutrients in their skin, so not only are we wasting food, but we're wasting the opportunity to boost our health.

Which is where *The Zero-Waste Kitchen* comes in. This book is all about helping you to save money, buy less, yet eat more (healthy food of course!), and do your bit for your family, environment and community. You'll discover lots of uses for food, around the home and in delicious meals, that you may otherwise put in the bin. There's advice on how to meal plan, and how to store and freeze ingredients and meals, so that you can enjoy them another time. Additionally, there are 44 delicious recipes to help you make the most out of all the ingredients in your fridge and cupboards, and eat well every day.

So, what are you waiting for? Let's get in the kitchen and start wasting less!

PART ONE: HOW TO BE WASTE-FREE IN THE KITCHEN

Making the necessary changes for a waste-free kitchen is relatively easy. Best of all, the whole family can get involved.

In this chapter you'll find advice on how to transform your kitchen habits and behaviours, from tips on shopping mindfully to reducing kitchen clutter, and how to store and reheat leftovers with confidence.

Once you've made these changes, you'll be well on your way to a kitchen that is sustainable and a conscience that is guilt-free.

CHANGING YOUR SHOPPING HABITS

Reducing the amount of food you waste at home begins by cutting down on the amount of food you buy, and how you cook this food. The following ideas are focused on how to start to reduce your overall waste, which means you'll throw less food away and also reduce your shopping bills.

Make a list

Before you go food shopping, take an inventory of what you already have in stock. This may mean you need to have a clear-out of your fridge and cupboards so that you know what food you already have. Some people keep a list on their fridge and add to it as they run out of a certain food – compiling their shopping list as the week goes by.

Make a meal plan

Knowing what you're going to cook each day can help you save time, money and eliminate waste. If you buy no more than what you expect to use, you are more likely to keep it fresh and use it all.

How to plan meals you'll eat

1 Look in your fridge or cupboard. What's languishing there that could be eaten? Take a look at the recipes (starting on page 54) to find out what you could make with that slightly soft bunch of carrots, for example. Write down any extra ingredients you need in order to make meals from these ingredients.

2 Write down a list of meals using the food already in your fridge, under the day you intend to cook and eat them.

3 List the ten most common meals you enjoy. Don't forget to ask the whole family, or your partner or flatmate(s) for their input. Specific meals for specific days of the week can help you plan: think meat-free Monday, taco Tuesday, fish and chips Friday – whatever you prefer.

4 Fill out your weekly menu, including all main meals and snacks. Don't forget to consider how many nights you may be eating out (bring any leftovers home), or the times you may have a large lunch and so may desire a lighter evening meal. And consider a "leftovers" menu. For instance, a delicious roast chicken and accompanying tray of vegetables can be used for soup, stir-fry, frittata, or lunches (with rice or pasta) over the following days; Bolognese can be turned into chilli or added to a baked potato for a delicious lunch; leftover lamb is ideal for a curry; excess fruit can be used up in a smoothie. Our recipe section is full of great ideas to help you use up leftovers.

5 Be realistic about your eating habits and adjust your purchases accordingly. For instance, if you always have several leftover bananas in your fruit bowl at the end of the week, either buy fewer or look at the different ways you can use them so that they don't go to waste.

6 Food that goes off quickly or has a shorter lifespan should of course be cooked or used as early as possible, so adjust your meal plan to reflect the use-by dates.

7 Once your meal plan is finalized, write your shopping list in full.

When to shop

We all know what can happen at the supermarket. We head there, shopping list in one hand, reusable bags in the other, determined to stick to our list "no matter what!" And then, suddenly, random items appear in our trolley, as we're enticed by reduced price stickers, special offers or the snacks next to the till.

Buying in this way is what is known as dynamic inconsistency – when we eat or buy for what we think we want, rather than what we know we need. This type of behaviour can occur regardless of whether you're shopping online or in person.

Some research shows that online shopping helps you avoid impulse purchasing by encouraging you to type your shopping list into the search bar. By sticking to the list you'll be less likely to add unneeded treats or ingredients. Some shopping websites encourage you to purchase food according to their online recipes – again, this can help you avoid adding unnecessary products as you're only buying the specific ingredients you need for that week's meal plan. However, if you don't like purchasing your food online, or it's not available to you, keep these points in mind:

- Try to avoid shopping when you're hungry. This is the most likely time for those unplanned items to jump into your trolley.

- Only go down the aisles where your essentials, e.g. fresh fruit, vegetables, bread, meat, poultry and frozen food, are situated.

- Buy your fruit loose, meat from the butcher and, if possible, nuts and seeds from a "refiller" shop which allows you to buy the specific amount you need. This type of "bespoke" shopping may take a little longer, but you'll be buying exactly what you need, rather than pre-packaged sizes which may be too large.

- Next head to the rice, pasta and pulses aisle. These foods are long lasting: provided you store them correctly, they're an ideal back-up and way to bulk up leftovers.

- Use the scales (if available) and try to limit the amount of packaging you're taking home with you by taking along your own reusable produce bags or containers.

Where to shop

Other than the major supermarkets and grocery stores, independent grocery stores, farmer's markets and "refiller" stores allow you to buy just what you need, and usually encourage you to bring your own string bags and storage containers to fill.

There are other benefits to shopping at your local farmer's market, butcher, fishmonger or greengrocer's: the produce is more likely to be organic, as many small-scale farmers use organic farming methods, and it will usually come from somewhere local, helping reduce the impact of transportation on the environment. The produce will also be less likely to be treated with chemicals in order to remain "fresh".

> Ask your stallholder for recipe ideas, especially for using leftovers. As they need to take home any unsold goods, these guys are the experts in finding other uses for whatever's left.

Buying in bulk – is it worth it?

It can be tempting to buy large quantities of a particular product if it's on sale. However, if it goes off or just takes up precious cupboard space, it's really just a waste of money.

Nevertheless, there are certain foods and products which tend to be cheaper when purchased in bulk and have a long shelf life. And when you buy in bulk there tends to be less fancy packaging, which means you're not paying over the odds for a product.

What to buy in bulk

Coffee beans – making your own coffee at home and using a "keep cup" is a great way to save money (and the environment, as you're not wasting a paper cup). Buy your coffee in bulk and store it in the freezer in its original packaging, if it's resealable, or an airtight container. It will keep for three to six months.

Nuts – buying your favourite nutty snacks in bulk works out a lot cheaper than purchasing smaller-sized portions. They will keep in the fridge in an airtight container for four months or in the freezer for six to twelve months.

Butter – if you're always running out of butter just when you've got your bake on, this is a simple way to cut down costs and have some to hand. Just buy the largest butter available and freeze in smaller-sized 50-g portions for up to six months.

Pasta – keep your dry pasta in an airtight container in a cool, dark cupboard and it will last up to two years.

Rice – a great dinner staple, rice lasts pretty much forever. Keep it alongside your pasta in an airtight container.

Cereal – your morning breakfast, such as oats, can be purchased in bulk and stored in an airtight container for six to eight months.

Laundry detergent – larger quantities are much cheaper per litre than smaller bottles and will keep forever.

STORING YOUR FOOD

It's tempting to just fling your shopping into your fridge and cupboards when you get home. However, taking time to sort and organize it will help in the long run, and cut down on waste. A clean and tidy fridge and cupboard will enable you to see what you already have, and help cut down on unnecessary purchases the next time you go shopping.

- **Work out a system that suits you and your lifestyle, such as keeping a list of what you have run out of. If your freezer is small, it can help to list whatever is already in there (meat, fish, leftovers) to help you plan your meals.**

- **If you have purchased grains, pasta or flour from a refill store, or just prefer to decant your ingredients, use labels to help you identify the containers' food at a glance. You can rewrite the contents and date as and when this is needed, and put the freshest food towards the back and the oldest to the front.**

STORING, REFRIGERATING AND FREEZING

Different food has different storage needs, so it's important to take the time to stow it away correctly.

Vegetables

Green leafy vegetables (think kale, lettuce, broccoli, celery) should always be stored in the fridge. Avoid excess moisture that can form on the produce by lining the crisper with a paper towel. Too much moisture can mean your favourite salad ingredients are being attacked by microbes, leaving you with a slimy, smelly mess.

Tip: Wash leaves before storing, cooking or making your salad or meal.

Do: Store green leafy veg in the plastic bags they were sold in or your reusable veg bags. Avoid airtight containers as condensation will build up and they will go off quicker.

Green beans, cucumbers, herbs need to be stored in the fridge – ideally in the crisper – after they've been thoroughly washed and dried.

Do: Remove the wrapping your cucumber is sold in. (And any plastic on other veg.) Wrap the cucumber in a clean dish towel or paper towel to keep out condensation. Only used half? Cover the cut end of a cucumber with a small piece of beeswax paper. Place beans and herbs in small plastic containers, for protection against ethylene gas.

WHAT IS ETHYLENE GAS?

Some fruits (and some vegetables) emit a gas called ethylene, which breaks down chlorophyll, the chemical that keeps plants green and helps them make energy. The riper the fruit or veg, the more ethylene gas it produces. This gas can then lead to nearby fruit and veg ripening more quickly.

Keep your **potatoes and yams** in a cool dark place – around 6–10°C is ideal. This is warmer than a refrigerator but not so hot that they'll go off quickly or start sprouting. Studies have found that keeping potatoes in a cool area will give them a shelf life three times longer than if they were stored at room temperature.

Remove your potatoes from any plastic and place in a brown paper bag or ventilated storage container.

Storing your potatoes in the dark also prevents them from turning green and developing what's called solanine. A high solanine content can cause nausea, vomiting and diarrhoea if you consume it in high quantities.

Carrots and other root veg should be stored in the refrigerator. If there's dirt on your root vegetables, you can leave it on until it's time to eat them. This helps preserve their crispness.

Don't cut or slice carrots unless you have an airtight container to store them in. They'll go dry and lose their rigidity. Do cut off the green leafy tops of carrots (if they have them still attached) but don't throw them away as they can be stored in airtight containers in the fridge for up to one week and used like herbs. Or chop them finely and place in an ice cube tray, along with some olive oil or water. Freeze and the ice cubes can be used in stocks, sauces or casseroles.

Fruit

Leave whole, but consider storing **strawberries, blueberries, and raspberries** in sealable containers (with built-in vents), or containers with fitted lids. Make sure they're not sitting in water, as this will just cause your fruit to become soggy and inedible. If your fruit was purchased prepacked in a container, you can leave it in this.

Some types of fruit continue to ripen after being picked – **stone fruit, pears, apples, kiwis, tomatoes and avocados** – so leave them on the kitchen bench. The cold air of a refrigerator can interrupt their ripening and affect the taste, colour and texture of the fruit.

Many fruits give off natural gases as they ripen, making other nearby produce spoil faster. Store **bananas, apples, and tomatoes** by themselves. Fruits should be kept separately from vegetables, so store in different drawers in your fridge.

Fruits with a high water content, such as **strawberries and tomatoes**, will lose their texture and firmness. They are ideal for smoothies or cooking in muffins (berries) or sauces (tomatoes) though, so freeze them if you intend to use them at a later date in this way.

Meat and poultry

All meat and poultry should be stored in clean, sealed containers (fridge or freezer).

Place meat and poultry at the bottom of the fridge. If there's a leak in the bag or container, it won't drip onto the produce on other shelves.

Keep cooked meat separate from raw meat and ready meals when storing.

Freeze meat as soon as you bring it home from the shop or butcher, or before its use-by date. Don't forget to label the container with the date you placed it into the freezer. Ideally, divide it into serving or cooking portions.

If you have thawed some meat only to realize that you're not going to cook it in the next couple of days, it is safe to refreeze it (as long as it was defrosted in the fridge). The meat may lose some of its taste and moisture but it will be fine to eat.

Meat or poultry on the bone should be defrosted overnight, so you will need to plan your meals ahead. When defrosting, the meat will release some liquid. Place the frozen bundle into a large bowl to prevent bacteria spreading over your countertop or onto other ingredients.

It may be simpler for you to defrost meat or poultry in a microwave. It's quicker and there's a reduced risk of bacteria forming.

Make sure you always cook meat thoroughly. It can be worthwhile buying a food thermometer so that you can check that the entire piece of meat is properly cooked.

When freezing meat or poultry, cover it completely and securely in food wrap, or in a glass container.

Date and label containers.

Keep for no longer than six months, as the quality will begin to deteriorate after three months.

If you do find meat or poultry that has been frozen for longer, defrost it, then marinate it and add lots of herbs and spices to help add flavour.

Fish

If you've defrosted a piece of fish then decide you don't want to cook it, don't refreeze it. Instead, store for up to 24 hours in the fridge, in an airtight container.

Frozen fish (and meat) can be defrosted, cooked, then refrozen once cooled. This is a good idea if you are doing some bulk cooking or want to use up leftovers for future meals.

Bread

Keep your bread in a breadbox – the larger the better to keep humidity levels low. Your favourite loaf can be stored in the freezer. If you've bought a whole loaf, consider slicing it before freezing, to make it easier to remove slices as needed. If you don't have a bread box you can store your loaf in the wrapping it came in.

Tip: If your baguette or uncut loaf has gone hard, spritz the crust lightly with water then place it into the oven for a minute or so to bring back some of the freshness.

Dairy and eggs

Cheese is best frozen when grated or chopped into small chunks. Generally, soft cheese shouldn't be frozen, while semi-hard cheeses can. Hard cheeses pick up lots of moisture when they are frozen so be sure to grate them first.

Store egg whites separately if you've used the yolks for baking. If you want to store your **eggs**, then beat them first before sealing them in an airtight container in the freezer. Boiled eggs can be frozen with the shell removed, but they do also last around two days in a fridge. These are great for salads, or snacks on the go.

Although **milk** is fine to freeze it can become lumpy when thawed, or full-fat milk can separate, which may slightly affect the taste. If you do freeze it make sure there is enough room in the container for it to expand. This goes for anything that's a liquid!

Sour cream can be frozen, but the texture changes considerably so you may only want to use it in this way when it's part of a recipe.

WHAT TO DO WITH LEFTOVERS

As different leftover food needs to be stored in different ways and kept for specific amounts of time, the rule of thumb is to store it in an airtight glass or plastic container in the refrigerator and eat it within two days.

Leaving cooked food on your countertop to cool before storing is a myth, and one that could be potentially harmful. Leaving food out at room temperature encourages bacteria to thrive. Initiate the two-hour rule: food should only be out for two hours before placing in the fridge or freezer.

What to store leftovers in

Plastic containers have suffered a backlash over the past few years (along with plastic bags, bottles and unnecessary packaging). This is mainly due to environmental reasons, as plastic has literally taken over the world. Just look at the facts:

- **We use around 5 trillion plastic bags every year, worldwide.**

- **Only 1–3 per cent of all plastics are recycled; the rest is thrown away.**

- **The Great Pacific Garbage Patch, a floating island of plastic that is in the ocean, is three times the size of France.**

- **The manufacture of plastics accounts for around eight per cent of the world's oil production**

- **90 per cent of the trash floating in our oceans is made of plastic.**

Health issues with plastic

According to Harvard Health, certain chemicals in plastic can leach out of the plastic into the food and beverages we consume. Research shows links between these chemicals, namely phthalates and bisphenol A, and health problems such as metabolic disorders and reduced fertility. And if you microwave your food in its plastic container – you may be receiving an even higher dose of potentially harmful chemicals.

What to use instead

Glass containers or BPA-free plastic containers with air vents are best to store your food, leftovers, or ingredients. Make sure the lid fits securely – not just to prevent leakages, but so bacteria can't build up. Glass or clear containers are best to store food or leftovers in, to help you see at a glance what they hold. Most glass is also oven- and microwave-proof, and dishwasher safe (there should be wavy lines on the bottom of the containers to indicate whether you can use them in the microwave). And you can reuse these containers over and over again. Best of all, you can put still-hot leftover food into them without worrying they'll melt (as you would with plastic).

Keep your empty jars – jars which once contained condiments are perfect for storing grains and seeds. Or you can make salads, puddings, juices or porridge (using up your leftovers) in them and carry them with you to work, school or as a snack on the go. They have a screw top lid which prevents leaking – and again, they're good for the environment.

If glass containers don't suit you, there are now many meal-prep style plastic containers available on the market (they tend to have a large squarish section for the main part of the meal, a smaller rectangle segment for extras). Look for the BPA-free sticker to ensure these don't contain nasty chemicals.

Canned food

Leftover tinned food shouldn't be stored in the open tin in the fridge. There have been some reported cases of botulism (a food-borne disease which causes serious illness) from cans that weren't sealed properly, plus canned foods are often highly perishable. Instead, pour the contents into a container and seal tightly. Wash and dry the tins – these can be used to grow herbs or seedlings as part of your kitchen garden. If you have no use for them, put them in the recycling.

The way you store your leftover food in the freezer will help extend its life and edibility. Place it in an airtight container (unsealed food will dry out). Don't forget to label the contents and date it – otherwise you'll end up with containers of frozen food with no idea what's inside and how long they've been there.

Batch cooking

If you're preparing a meal to eat at a later date, err on the side of caution when dividing up the portion sizes to freeze. Smaller portions can be bulked out with carbohydrates (such as lentils or beans) or a salad.

Meat

If you're going to freeze leftover meat, it's a good idea to either shred or chop it before storing. Date and label the container and use within two months. When you decide to use it in the future, use some stock to soften it and add some herbs to replace any lost flavours.

Will my rice still be nice?

Leftover rice is one of those ingredients that gets parcelled up and stored in the refrigerator, rarely to be used again. While government and food safety guidelines say that rice left standing at room temperature is at risk of growing *Bacillus cereus* spores, a bacterium that can cause food poisoning, vomiting or diarrhoea, it can be eaten safely as leftovers by following these steps:

- As soon as rice has been cooked and has stopped steaming (and no longer than 1½ hours after cooking), put it in an airtight container and place in the fridge. Consume within two to three days of cooking.

- You can store cooked rice in the freezer. Follow the same storage instruction and eat within two weeks, to prevent freezer burn. (Don't forget to date your container!)

- When it is time to enjoy your leftover rice, add a splash of water to it and reheat it until it's piping hot. Do not thaw it first.

TOP TIP

Avoid leftovers by getting your serving sizes right. Ideally, cook 60 g of rice per person, but your serving size may vary according to your needs, or whether you're planning on using rice in the following day's meal. (If you have leftover rice go to page 53 for some ways to use it up.)

SERVING SIZES

The amount we eat has a lot to do with the amount of food we waste. Rather than buy what we need on a daily basis, we instead buy for what we immediately need AND for what we may want at a later date. And all this extra food is causing health issues.

Worldwide, we have an obesity problem. In 2016, more than 1.9 billion adults, 18 years and older, were overweight. Of these, over 650 million were obese.

According to WHO, portion sizes of not only pre-packed or takeaway meals, but also home-cooked meals have increased substantially over the past few decades.

One study found that our typical portion size and servings of breads, cereals, meat and starchy vegetables were a massive 160 per cent larger than the recommended servings.

This wouldn't be such a problem if we were eating more fruit and veg. But it seems that as our portions of fattening food have increased (up to 400 per cent in some cases), we're serving ourselves up to 90 per cent less fruits and non-starchy vegetables such as broccoli and leafy greens.

Mindful eating tips

To help reduce the amount of food you have left on your plate – which may then be thrown away as waste – try these tips to ensure you're only serving yourself the amount of food you need and will eat.

- **Serve meals on smaller plates.**

- **Serve meals in the kitchen rather than allowing people to help themselves at the table, when portion sizes could easily get out of hand.**

- **Eat at the table, not in front of the television or a screen. This means you'll pay more attention to what you're eating and your satiety.**

- **Make sure your main meals consist of half green or salad vegetables (not including starchy ones like potatoes).**

- **You don't have to clean your plate; stop when you feel full. Keep any leftovers for the next day's meal (see the recipe section for some ideas).**

- **When eating out, if there's a choice, opt for the smaller size or ask for a "doggie bag" to take leftovers home for later. You'll have a ready-made lunch or dinner for you to enjoy another day and reduce the waste of the restaurant too.**

Portion sizes: a guide

There's a simple way to reduce your portion sizes – by using your own hand as a guide.

Palm of your hand
Meat including steak, chicken and lamb

Size of your entire hand
Fish

The size of your closed fist
Rice, grains, pasta, bread – use a half-cup measure to scoop it out of the pan
Beans and legumes

Two cupped hands
Non-starchy vegetables such as leafy greens

One cupped hand
Starchy vegetables such as potato, sweet potato and corn
Fruit

Dairy is a bit tricky to show with a hand but a portion is about 200 ml milk, two slices of cheese or 125 ml yoghurt.

NB: How many servings you need from each food group depends on your age and level of activity. Pregnant or lactating women may need more and older people may need less.

COMMON FOOD AND GROCERY SHOPPING QUESTIONS

What do use-by dates mean?

Some products can be eaten after their use-by date, but it depends on the contents. It is important to note that there are two types of time stamps on your food. One is the use-by date: this is the date that your food should be eaten and tends to appear on products that expire quickly, such as milk. The other, "best before" date is the recommended date you should have eaten that food by – any time after and the food may lose its nutrients or you may experience a loss of taste, but it is still edible if it's not showing signs that it has gone off.

My power's gone. Do I have to throw everything out?

If you have a power failure, it's important to know the rules when it comes to storing, thawing and eating the food in your fridge and freezer. The best way to keep your food safe if the electricity is off for a few hours is to keep the door shut, to keep the cool air inside and stable.

If your fridge or freezer loses electricity, the temperature inside starts to rise. When this happens, microbes begin growing on food, which can make it inedible and unsafe to eat. If the power is out for longer than four hours (and the fridge temperature has risen by more than five degrees in two hours), the food either needs to be eaten immediately or thrown away.

Can I reuse my resealable bag?

Many people throw resealable bags away after one use, adding to the world's already enormous plastic waste pile. These bags can be reused: just wash them in warm water with soap and dry thoroughly, inside out. To ensure they are completely dry, stretch the bags across your taps or drainer.

Top tip: If the bag has contained raw meat or food that has turned mouldy, you should dispose of it.

Environment tip: Rather than adding to the plastic mountain, invest in some silicon sealable sandwich and storage bags. They can be used many times and are suitable for freezer use.

How can I reduce my supermarket packaging waste?

For low-waste brownie points, take cotton string bags and select your preferred amount of loose produce from the supermarket rather than the double-wrapped in rigid plastic option. If you do have excess plastic wrapping, reuse it, or send it for recycling.

Is online shopping better for the environment?

There are several benefits to doing your shopping from the comfort of your own home, but the downside is that you might be increasing your carbon footprint via transportation of goods. There is no black or white answer to this question, rather each individual should weigh up the pros and cons of how they get their food. For example, if you use public transport or go by foot, then ordering a delivery will put an extra van on the road. However, if you travel by car to a supermarket, then it may be better for the environment to get your groceries ordered to your home as a delivery van will also be going to other homes to deliver food nearby. To make sure you are being as environmentally friendly as possible when you do an online shop, consider the following:

- **Meal planning means you shouldn't have to shop more than once a week (or two if you cook in bulk). If you need to "top up" your groceries (with items such as milk, bread, etc.), use a local shop you can walk or cycle to.**

- **Fruit and veg boxes delivered from your local grower are a great way to support smaller businesses, plus the food will be fresher as it will have travelled a shorter distance.**

- **Consider clubbing together with your neighbours to buy goods online. This way delivery is to one address.**

That vegetable looks strange – should I still eat it?

So-called "ugly" fruit and vegetables – the produce rejected by shops and consumers for not being "perfect" enough – is a big contributor to our food waste mountain. About 20–40 per cent of fruit and veg is wasted worldwide before it even reaches us – mainly due to the strict cosmetic standards of stores and shoppers alike. However, our desire for perfect-looking food is purely superficial. Misshapen, twisted or unusually shaped fruit and vegetables are just as nutritious and delicious as their more attractive family members. Some research says that "ugly" fruit and vegetables may even be better for us. Research has shown that imperfect produce, such as grapes and apples, contains higher levels of antioxidants – the good stuff that helps our bodies fight disease.

More and more supermarkets and produce delivery companies are offering "ugly" fruit and vegetables at cheaper prices than their better-looking counterparts. If you really don't want "ugly" fruit and veg on your plate, there are other ways to use them. Make the most of your misshapen vegetables by using them in juices, smoothies, soups or casseroles. Once a piece of fruit or veg is peeled, chopped or blended, there's not much difference between the perfect and imperfect version. So why not save the planet and your pocket?

GROWING FRUIT AND VEGETABLES FROM SCRAPS AND SEEDS

The wonderful thing about fruit and veg leftovers is that you can use them to start your own indoor or outdoor garden, and it is extremely simple.

Cabbage

Place leftover cabbage leaves in a bowl of water and leave in a sunny spot. Replace the water every day until new roots appear. Plant the leaves into a compost-filled pot (at least 30-cm diameter) or into a garden bed until the cabbage fully grows. You can then take those leaves to repeat the growing process.

Celery

You know that end part of the celery nobody eats? You can use this to grow more celery.

Take the bottom two centimetres of the celery base and place in a shallow bowl of water.

Spray the tops of the celery sticks every day to ensure the stump doesn't dry out and replace the water in the bowl every couple of days. When the new root system begins to grow, plant it into a compost-filled pot or in the ground.

Herbs

If you already have a herb garden, you can use what's already planted to create further plants. (If not, you can either invest in a herb garden or ask a kind friend to share some cuttings with you.) Snip the cutting at the area where sections of the plant meet and place the cut segment into a jar of water. Replace the water every few days until roots begin to grow. Then plant in a pot or the ground, watering regularly.

Garlic

Plant a garlic clove into soil – either in a garden bed or pot – point-side up. If you have more than one clove, plant them 10 to 15 cm apart. They'll take around a year to grow and should be planted just before winter begins.

Ginger

Soak the root of the ginger in warm water for 12 hours. Then plant it sideways in a large pot so it has plenty of room to grow, covering it completely with soil. Place on the windowsill, balcony or anywhere it will catch the sun. Water regularly to keep the soil moist. Ginger takes several months to grow, so plant throughout the year to ensure you have a regular supply.

Leeks and spring onions

You know the white roots of these veg? They can be used to grow more of your must-have ingredients. Place the base of the leek or spring onion in a clear jar or cup and fill it with water. Place in a sunny place – such as your windowsill – and change the water every other day. Within a few weeks you'll have new veg to add to your cooking.

Lettuce and bok choy

Like celery, the base of the lettuce usually gets thrown away or added to the compost. This tip will ensure you'll have fresh lettuce leaves within a fortnight. Just take the base of a head of lettuce and place, cut side up, in a bowl of water (and replace this every couple of days). By the time two weeks have passed new leaves will have grown, which you can then use in salads. Compost the entire plant after you've used all the leaves.

Peppers

Also known as capsicum, these veg are great as snacks, in cooking and, best of all, are easily grown from seed. The next time you use up a pepper, save the seeds from its centre. Plant them directly into seedling containers (you can use tins or empty yoghurt pots) and water regularly. Keep indoors until a shoot emerges, then transfer to your garden or a bigger pot.

Potatoes and sweet potatoes or yams

We've all gone to our potato bag only to find some weird waving green shoots emerging from the spuds. Rather than growing potatoes in your cupboard, plant them in the ground. Firstly, cut up 5-cm pieces and leave them out to dry (for around two days). Plant in early spring for best results.

Strawberries

Cut the outer skin from the berry, or you can use tweezers to dig out the tiny seeds. Plant the skin or seeds in soil in a container large enough to hold a strawberry plant and place in a sunny area. Water regularly, being careful not to overwater the soil. Once the sprouts begin to grow you can transfer it to the ground or continue to let it grow in a pot (just make sure you've chosen one big enough – around 25 cm in diameter is ideal).

Tomatoes

Tomatoes are so easy to grow, so choose an area where you're happy for them to continue reproducing every year. All you need to do is to keep the seeds from a fully grown tomato and plant these into a small pot (a yoghurt pot or tin) filled with soil. When the small plant begins to grow, transfer this into the ground. You may need to use wiring or bamboo poles to hold up the vines as they get bigger and heavier.

Pumpkins

These are the easiest veg of all to grow. Be warned – they can take up a lot of ground and require a lot of space so that the pumpkins don't rot under the leaves. You can plant the seeds of a pumpkin directly into garden soil.

TOP TIP

It can be difficult to remember what needs watering when. Group the plants that need daily watering in one area and label them; do the same with the ones that need watering every few days and set a reminder on your phone or calendar. As a rule of thumb, they should be watered when the soil turns dry.

HOW TO MAKE A COMPOST HEAP

Instead of sending your kitchen and garden waste to landfill, make your own nutritiously rich compost heap:

- **Buy or make your own compost bin (the bigger, the better).**

- **Find an area of your garden that is shaded; placing the compost bin straight on top of soil is best, but if your garden is paved, put a bottom layer of soil down.**

- **Add up to 50 per cent of "green" material – including food waste (not meat!), grass clippings, leafy plants, weeds – and the rest "brown" material – e.g. prunings, hedge trimmings, leaves, paper or card (in small pieces), plant stems, straw and woodchips.**

- **Turn the waste frequently (every week) to allow air into it.**

- **You should get good results within six months to two years.**

COMPOSTING – TOP TIPS

- Keep the heap moist and loose.
- If the heap becomes slimy and smelly, there is too much "green" material (e.g. grass cuttings) and it is too moist – counter the problem by adding more "brown" material (e.g. dead leaves) and covering the heap to protect it from the rain.
- If the heap is too dry and doesn't look like it's breaking down, try adding more green waste to it and a little water.
- If your heap is attracting flies, make sure your kitchen waste is well hidden under other waste.

PART TWO: THE A–Z OF LEFTOVERS

It's often easy to accumulate leftovers, but difficult to know how to reuse them to make other tasty meals. In this section you'll discover lots of ideas, tips and tricks to get you started. Handily laid out as an A–Z, this guide will be your one-stop shop for waste-free mealtimes.

A

Apples: Use bruised or slightly soft apples in juices or desserts, such as crumbles or pies. Drying leftover fruit is an ideal way to enjoy a healthy snack. Slice the apple and bake in the bottom of the oven at 160°C for 15–20 minutes. Sprinkle some cinnamon, nutmeg or brown sugar on top for extra sweetness.

Aubergine: Thinly slice any leftover aubergine. Soak up excess moisture with a paper towel and place in the oven at 180°C for 20–30 minutes, or until golden. Add a drizzle of honey on top for added sweetness. Or dip slices in egg, flour and breadcrumbs for a wonderfully crunchy dish. Just bake in the oven for 25 minutes at 180°C. Leftover aubergine can also be added to curries or casseroles for extra goodness.

Avocado: Avocados can be tricky. One moment they're as hard as a rock, the next they're brown and inedible. Mash avocados, even the brown bits, with some lemon, salt, pepper and a little olive oil for a tasty dip. Serve with some carrot or celery sticks. To help mashed avocados last longer, leave the stone in and squeeze over some lemon juice to help stop it turning brown.

B

Bananas: Store brown or browning bananas in the freezer. They're perfect for smoothies, muffins, pancakes, banana ice cream (which can also use up leftover milk, or milk that's about to turn) or banana bread. There's no need to waste banana skin. Some people swear by the healing power of banana skins to remove warts and verrucas. Others claim that a frozen banana may help reduce the severity of a headache as your skin absorbs the potassium in the banana, which can alleviate the pain. A banana skin placed against the area containing a splinter can draw it to the surface. You can also mash an overripe banana and apply it to wet hair for a nourishing treatment.

Basil: If you've bought a basil plant for a specific recipe and have some leaves or stalks left over, use them up as toppings on pizzas, pasta, cocktails, salads or in sandwiches.

Beetroot: Roasted beetroot is a wonderful health-boosting dish. Even older beetroot is just as delicious baked for 40 minutes at 160°C. Alternatively, juice beetroot along with carrot, apple and celery – it's an ideal way to start the day.

Blueberries: These blue powerhouses can go off quickly, so freeze them (or half the punnet) after purchasing if you're not using them straight away. Frozen, they're a tasty, but low-calorie snack. Older blueberries are ideal to use in pancakes, muffins or cakes, or whizzed up in a juice.

Bok choy: Even old, limp leaves can be used in a stir fry. Or add to a noodle soup alongside other veg.

Bread: If you're sick of throwing bread away, then a little bit of prep can save it from the garbage. It's easy to turn stale bread into breadcrumbs (and cheaper than buying your own), or fry bread in oil, salt, onion salt and garlic for croutons to place on top of your soup.

If you cut the crusts off your sandwiches, roll the crusts together and secure with a skewer. Fry in butter, sugar and cinnamon for mini cinnamon rolls. Bread puddings are also a delicious after-dinner treat (check out our recipe on page 74).

To preserve unused bread just slice it and store it in the freezer in a tea towel or plastic bag.

It's also handy to help remove excess fat or oil from soups and stews – just lightly pat the surface of the soup or stew to skim off excess fat or oil.

One unusual tip: stale bread can remove smudges and marks from your walls.

Broccoli: When the tips of broccoli began to turn yellow or brown, it's an indication that your broccoli is losing nutrients. Chop and remove the florets, blanch in boiling water and freeze to use later in soups, casseroles or a pasta bake. The stems are filled with goodness – use in a slaw, noodle soup or stir fry.

C

Carrots: Grate and mix with other remaining veg such as broccoli stalks, celery or cabbage for a summery slaw dish. They're also perfect for cakes, muffins, casseroles or soup.

Cauliflower: Slice the stalk thinly to use in a stir fry. Any florets remaining can be roasted with paprika and olive oil for a crunchy snack or blitzed for a healthy "rice" option.

Celery: Juice along with carrot, ginger and apple for a sweet start to the day or add to salad for additional crunch. Celery that has wilted can be (temporarily) perked up by soaking stems overnight in cold water. Add to Bolognese sauce or soups such as potato or broccoli.

Cheese: Grate your cheese and freeze it in an airtight container. It can be kept for up to two months before it begins to lose its taste and texture.

Chicken skin: Remove the skin from the meat and chop into small pieces. Preheat the oven to 190°C. Line a baking tray with baking paper or parchment. Arrange the chicken skin evenly on the paper, skin side up. Bake for 40 minutes or until the skin has become crisp and golden. Use a paper towel to soak up excess fat. Enjoy on its own or on top of steamed vegetables as a salty topping.

Courgette: Roast in the oven for 20–25 minutes at 180°C with olive oil, salt and pepper. You may need to experiment with the length of time you roast your courgette depending on whether you like it al dente or slightly softer. Mash roasted courgettes and add to leftover mashed potato for fritters, or salmon or tuna cakes. Soak in egg, flour and breadcrumbs and pop in the oven for crunchy courgette chips. Use a spiralizer to create courgette spaghetti, which can be cooked in boiling water (in place of wheat-based spaghetti), or stir fry the noodles.

D

Dates: Use up remaining dates in oatmeal, porridge, cookies, pilaf or salads. With just a little more effort you can enjoy stuffed dates with goat's cheese and almonds, or drizzle with honey and wrap them in prosciutto. Place in the oven and bake for 10–15 minutes at 190°C.

E

Eggs: If you've separated your eggs (to use in baking, for example), and you're left with the whites, you can quickly use them up by mixing them into a stir fry. They'll bind the ingredients together and give you some extra protein. If you have several whites use them for delicious meringues or cake toppings. Egg whites will keep in the fridge for two days, or they can be frozen. If the situation is reversed and you have egg yolks sitting around, just add a splash of milk for scrambled egg or omelette. You can throw in some leftover spinach, tomato or peppers too for a good fridge clear-out. Or use the yolk to bind together mince when making burgers or meatballs. It gives them an extra juicy texture.

You can use eggshells in your garden to deter pests such as slugs and snails, or sprinkle crushed eggshells around your tomato plants, they'll add calcium as they compost.

And if you want to grow your own seedlings, don't waste money on special pots. Instead, place the big half of an eggshell into the egg carton. Fill with compost and add your chosen seeds. Move to the garden once the shoot has appeared (depending on the plant).

F

Figs: If you have some figs languishing, add them to porridge, salad, or a stir fry for sweetness. For a sweet-tasting smoothie, add figs to a chopped banana, tablespoon of yoghurt and 60 ml (4 tablespoons) milk. Blend until smooth.

G

Garlic: Even garlic that has dried out can still be used – think anything that's going to simmer or cook slowly, such as soup, stocks, curries, stew or casseroles. If your garlic has sprouted, fry the shoots in olive oil, salt and pepper. Use them as toppings for soup, salads or a stir fry.

H

Herbs: Chop herbs and freeze them in bags or containers. Or, if you're intending on using them in stews, casseroles or soups, place some chopped herbs at the bottom of an ice-tray and add some water, then freeze. Don't forget the stalks – add to a dressing or stir fry.

J

Juniper berries: Add to butter and garlic cloves to use as a sauce to accompany beef, duck, pork or lamb. Or fry leftover juniper berries and use alongside potatoes or cabbage for a delicious side dish.

K

Kale: Roast wilted, tired kale for a wonderfully crunchy snack. Either drizzle with olive oil or use olive oil spray (which doesn't weigh the leaves down as much). Crunchy kale can then be used in salads, stir fries, pizza toppings, or roast veg. Or just use any excess in soups, casseroles, or sauces. If you don't mind the slightly bitter taste, juice it along with celery, apple and ginger. A squeeze of lemon after blitzing can help lessen the bitter taste.

L

Lemons: Squeeze some lemon juice in a cup of hot water and drink first thing in the morning – it's said to help digestion. Several drops of lemon, along with mustard, olive oil, honey and seasoning are a perfect dressing for salads. Or add to roasted vegetables – it helps reduce excess greasiness if you've overdone the oil. Zest lemons into salads, sauces, dressings, on top of cake icing, in muesli or stir fries.

They're also a secret weapon when it comes to cleaning. Lemons act as a natural "bleach" to help cut through dirt and grime. Try sprinkling baking soda over shower tiles or in the bathtub and use the cut side of a lemon to scrub away the grime. Or place a couple of lemon peels into the cutlery drawer of your dishwasher to help remove grease. Remaining droplets of juice can be utilized to banish stains on the underarms of clothing – just rub the juice into the offending area and leave overnight before washing. If your chopping boards are a little whiffy, rub the cut side of a lemon over the surface to remove any lingering odours. It will also remove odours from your hands – use after cutting onions and garlic. Throw any leftover rinds into your fireplace for a lovely, citrusy scent. If your cat (or the neighbourhood feline gang) is getting into your garden, scatter lemon peels in the garden for a natural cat repellent.

Lettuce: Perk up a wilted lettuce leaf by soaking the leaves in ice water for a few minutes. Then put into a salad spinner to dry. Eating lettuce in a hot dish may seem slightly strange, but many French recipes do this – add to a chicken casserole, stir fry or pea soup.

M

Mayonnaise: There's always a couple of spoonfuls of mayo left at the bottom of the jar that can be put to good use. Don't double up your spreads – use mayonnaise in place of butter rather than using both (it'll save calories too) on your sandwiches, or in mashed potatoes. Add to avocados for a creamy dip, served with crackers, celery or carrot sticks.

Meat: When using up leftover meat don't be afraid to experiment. Pasta bakes are always a tasty meal, and they transport well, so they're an ideal lunch to take to the office.

If you have leftover potatoes or vegetables, you can easily make another meal out of them. Simply mash them together, add some stock to the meat and layer the mash on top. Sprinkle with cheese and breadcrumbs and pop your pie in the oven until it's browned on top and piping hot all the way through. Add leftover meat to a salad but don't use it as the "hero" ingredient. Instead, cook up some rice, couscous or noodles and add a lot of vegetables. Your extra meat is just that – "extra" – not a main ingredient. Leftover meat is also a great way to make a pie, or individual pies, for the whole family to enjoy. You can make your own pastry or use shop-bought puff pastry.

Mushrooms: Dry your old mushrooms by placing them in the oven and baking, or simply leave them out to dry in the sunshine. Then store in a jar and use for extra flavour in stocks, soups or casseroles. Dried mushrooms are also ideal for risotto (see page 86 for recipe).

N

Nectarines: If you have one or two nectarines left over, use them on top of muesli, porridge or in a juice or smoothie. They're also a sweet addition to salads, especially those made with chicken or lamb.

O

Olives: Add a couple of olives to your pizza toppings, salads or soups. They add a wonderfully tangy and unexpected flavour. If you have quite a lot of olives left over and are unsure what to do with them, turn them into a paste, along with some olive oil, a squeeze of lemon and garlic. Spread on toast or serve as a dip.

P

Pasta: To avoid wasting pasta always measure your portions out carefully before cooking. But if you have cooked too much there is so much you can do with it. Add it to frittatas, muffins or a quiche. If you need to add some life to your pasta, heat it on a hot skillet, rather than in the microwave. Just add some olive oil, garlic paste or cloves along with some sage. This will give the pasta a little crunch.

Peppers: Chop or slice any remaining part of the peppers (avoiding the seeds) and add to pizza toppings, salads, tomato-based sauces, pasta-based dishes, stir fries, soups or casseroles. Peppers can also help clear problematic skin – juice along with a carrot and apple for a healthy morning drink.

Plums: Plums are like avocados – the moment you turn your back on them they become squishy and overripe. Mash them and serve on top of muesli or porridge with some yoghurt. If you have a large glut of plums you can boil them with some sugar and lemon to make a compote or turn them into mouth-watering cakes. Plum crumble is a delicious dessert too.

R

Rice: It's imperative to store cooked rice correctly to avoid food poisoning. See page 23 for advice. If you have only a small amount of rice left over, add a beaten egg, spring onions and ham for a delicious breakfast rice patty.

Risotto: Extra risotto can be repurposed as arancini balls, which are ideal for lunchboxes or snacks. See page 68 for recipe.

Roast potatoes: Cold roast potatoes are perfect in salads, or add them to your curry, soups (broccoli soup is wonderful with added potato) or slice into small cubes and refry to enjoy as especially crunchy chips.

Rocket: If your rocket is past its best, scatter on top of a pizza around five minutes before it's fully cooked, or include in a tomato-based sauce for an additional peppery taste. Or if you're making your own pesto, rocket can be included alongside basil leaves.

S

Satsumas and oranges: Simply juice any excess fruit and mix with yoghurt for a sweet, but sharp addition to muesli or porridge. Use instead of, or as well as, lemon in dressings. Or add to salads – they're delicious with leftover roast chicken salad.

Spaghetti: Don't throw away cooked spaghetti. Instead, chop it into smaller pieces and use in minestrone, tomato or chicken soup.

Spinach: Wilted spinach (that doesn't smell) is still edible and ideal for casseroles, soups, Bolognese sauce, lasagne or pizza toppings.

Sponge: Stir leftover cake into slightly melted ice cream and freeze. This will keep for months.

Stock: Freezing stock in ice cubes is ideal for future use. Then when you need a small amount of stock to add to soups, sauces or gravy, you can just add a cube.

T

Toast: If there's some spare bits of toast left from breakfast (even if it's the crust), chop into squares and fry in olive oil and seasoning. Then add as croutons on top of soup.

Tomatoes: An excess of tomatoes is a great excuse to make your own tomato sauce. Just add onion, garlic and basil and use for pizza toppings, Bolognese sauce, lasagne – any pasta recipe. Freeze for use in future recipes.

W

Watermelon: Juice watermelon for a delicious morning drink. Add coconut water or just drink neat with some ice and mint. Add some ice to turn it into a granita – just freeze until you're ready. If your watermelon is looking a little old, put it on the barbecue and grill it. Turn leftover watermelon into salsa and use in salads or as a dip. Or juice it until smooth, add some tomato sauce and coat chicken drumsticks with it. Bake in the oven and enjoy!

Wheat biscuits: Crushed wheat biscuits are perfect to use instead of breadcrumbs on chicken or fish.

Wine: Pour it into ice cube trays and freeze. You can then add to gravy or sauces. Better yet, you can add it to wine-based summer punches. This way you'll chill your wine without diluting it (compared to using water-based ice cubes).

Y

Yoghurt: Those few dribs and drabs of yoghurt at the bottom of the tub do well in a dressing. Just add some lemon juice and herbs. Yoghurt is also ideal to marinate chicken wings or drumsticks. Make the most of any stray carrots, peppers or celery and use as dippers in a yoghurt, cucumber and mint combination. Yoghurt can be used instead of eggs or butter if you're baking and are running short. If your curry is too hot, add some yoghurt to cool the hot spices down.

PART THREE: RECIPES FOR LEFTOVERS

It's time to get creative with your leftovers! The following recipes are based on the most common food leftovers – they're simple, easy to follow, and designed to help you use up remaining foods and ingredients so that they don't go to waste. Most of the recipes can be frozen (unless indicated) – if there are possible substitutes (such as adding a can of lentils to your Bolognese sauce to pad it out) this will also be suggested. In many cases the serving sizes are for just one person, so you can adjust as necessary. Many of these recipes (unless specified) suggest using non-specific types of food, e.g. cheese, milk, butter – this is so you can use whatever's available in your fridge or cupboards, rather than going out and buying, for example, full-fat milk when you usually drink semi-skimmed.

Use the recipes as a base for further experimentation – depending on the amount of leftovers you have of a certain ingredient, you could turn it into another meal (such as leftover roast chicken), or another serving to be enjoyed at a later date. Enjoy experimenting and let's get cooking!

CONVERSIONS AND MEASUREMENTS

All the conversions in the tables below are close approximates, which have been rounded up or down. When using a recipe, always stick to one unit of measurement and do not alternate between them.

Metric	Imperial	Metric	Imperial
10 g	½ oz	150 g	5 oz
25 g	1 oz	175 g	6 oz
40 g	1½ oz	200 g	7 oz
50 g	2 oz	225 g	8 oz
60 g	2½ oz	250 g	9 oz
75 g	3 oz	275 g	10 oz
110 g	4 oz	350 g	12 oz
125 g	4½ oz	450 g	1 lb

Metric	Imperial (UK)
30 ml	1 fl oz
60 ml	2 fl oz
125 ml	4 fl oz
250 ml	9 fl oz
375 ml	13 fl oz
500 ml	18 fl oz
1 litre	35 fl oz

Gas Mark	Celsius	Fahrenheit
1	140	275
2	150	300
3	170	325
4	180	350
5	190	375
6	200	400
7	220	425
8	230	450
9	245	475
10	260	500

LEFTOVER PASTA, RICE AND BREAD

If you've got too much bread, cooked pasta or rice, don't worry. There are so many ways to use up these leftovers – all you need is a little imagination. Many of the recipes here can also be frozen – ideal for lunch or an easy dinner. These recipes are all one serving unless otherwise stated.

Before using leftover pasta in the following recipes, place in a colander and pour boiling water over the pasta, or reheat it in the microwave.

If you're using rice you've already cooked, make sure you heat it properly in the microwave. See page 24 for instructions.

CHEESY CRUNCHY PASTA BAKE (V)

Turn your leftover pasta, kale, cheese AND bread into this delicious comfort meal.

Method

Heat the oven to 200°C. Revive the leftover pasta by pouring boiling water over it or reheating it in the microwave. Roughly chop the kale (both leaves and stem) and add to a frying pan along with the olive oil and salt and pepper. Fry on a medium heat for one to two minutes, or until the leaves begin to wilt. Place the kale into a food processor, with a dribble of milk. Blitz for 30 seconds. Pour over the pasta.

For the white sauce:
Melt the butter in a saucepan and add the flour. Stir to form a paste. Pour the remaining milk in gradually, stirring continuously until the sauce is thickened and coats the back of the spoon. Add the grated cheese and stir until melted. Pour the sauce over the kale and pasta and stir well. Sprinkle the breadcrumbs over the top and put the dish into the oven. Bake for 20 minutes or until the breadcrumbs have turned golden brown. Serve immediately. Add some shredded basil on top if you prefer.

Serves

2

Ingredients

200 g leftover pasta
40 g kale (leftover spinach will also work)
1 tbsp olive oil
Salt and pepper
250 ml milk, plus a little extra
40 g unsalted butter
120 g grated cheese
2 tbsp plain flour
2 tbsp breadcrumbs (you can use up slightly stale bread, including the crusts, for this)
Shredded basil, for garnish

SPAGHETTI CARBONARA

Use up those last pieces of spaghetti and bacon with this delicious Friday night treat. Add some spinach for some extra green goodness.

Method

Revive leftover spaghetti by pouring boiling hot water over it or reheating it in the microwave for around 2 minutes. Add some olive oil to a frying pan on a medium heat. Add the bacon and fry for around three minutes or until golden. Add the garlic and onion and fry briefly.

Pour in the wine and cook until it is almost completely evaporated.

Stir in the grated pecorino, season with salt and pepper, and add around 115 ml of hot water. Stir in the pasta.

Crack the egg and add it to the mixture, stirring until completely combined.

Stir in the parsley, if using, then serve topped with shaved Parmesan if you have some to hand.

Serves

1

Ingredients

100 g leftover spaghetti
½ tbsp olive oil
80 g bacon diced very finely
1 clove garlic, minced
1 onion, diced very finely
1 tbsp white wine
60 g grated pecorino, or other strong-flavoured cheese
Salt and pepper
1 egg
Handful of parsley leaves, chopped finely (optional)
Shaved Parmesan, to serve (optional)

CAULIFLOWER PASTA

A great dish to use up leftover pasta and cauliflower. Add spinach, broccoli or meat if desired.

Method

Cook the cauliflower florets in a large pan of boiling salted water for about four minutes until tender. Scoop the cauliflower out of the pan, drain and set aside, and reserve the water.

Heat the olive oil in a large pan, add the onion and cook over a medium heat until tender.

Add the garlic and chilli and cook for another minute.

Add the raisins and pine nuts to the pan and cook until the pine nuts are toasted and lightly golden.

Add the cauliflower, tomato paste and bay leaf to the pan along with 50 ml of the cauliflower cooking water. Season and cook over a low–medium heat for about 5 minutes.

Revive the leftover pasta then tip it into the saucepan with the cauliflower sauce. Add the lemon juice, chopped parsley and stir to combine. Add some of the reserved water if needed.

Serve immediately.

Serves

1

Ingredients

¼ cauliflower, chopped into small florets

1 tbsp olive oil

1 small onion, finely chopped

1 garlic clove, crushed

Pinch of crushed dried chilli

15 g raisins

15 g pine nuts

1 tsp tomato paste

1 bay leaf

80–100 g leftover pasta

Salt and pepper

1 tsp lemon juice

2 tsp flat leaf parsley, chopped

SPICY SALAMI PASTA SALAD

A simple yet delicious pasta dish that bursts with flavour. It's ideal for lunch or bulk it out for dinner with a side salad.

Method

Heat the oil in a small frying pan over a medium heat.

Add the salami and cook for 30 seconds on each side, or until browned. Remove from the pan.

Add the garlic and sauté for one minute, or until tender. Then add the tomatoes and sauté for three minutes.

Add the olives and stir gently before adding the salami and parsley.

Run the leftover pasta under boiling water or reheat in the microwave for 2 minutes. Mix the pasta in with the other ingredients until it's coated well.

Season with salt and pepper and serve with a sprinkle of Parmesan, if desired.

Serves

1

Ingredients

2 tsp olive oil

80 g spicy salami, sliced

3 cherry tomatoes, halved

1 tsp garlic paste (or 1 garlic clove, minced)

10 pitted olives

Coarsely chopped fresh flat-leaf parsley

100 g leftover pasta

Salt and pepper

Parmesan as desired

LEFTOVER PASTA FRITTATA

This is a simple way to use up leftover pasta, the dregs of pasta sauce and eggs. Add any scraps of spinach, kale or broccoli if you have some.

Method

Place the spaghetti into a saucepan with a little of the olive oil over medium heat or run under boiling water to revive it.

In a mixing bowl, add the egg and cheese, saving a teaspoon of Parmesan for serving, and season well. Stir so that all the ingredients are combined, then stir in the pasta.

In a small frying pan melt the remaining olive oil and butter. When slightly bubbling, pour the pasta mixture into the pan and press down to create a flat cake. Fry each side evenly until golden brown. Serve sprinkled with a teaspoon of Parmesan.

Makes

1 frittata

Ingredients

200 g leftover spaghetti
1 tbsp olive oil
3 eggs, beaten
60 g Parmesan cheese, grated
Salt and pepper
15 g butter

SALMON PASTA SALAD

This is a wonderfully tasty dish, great for a summer lunch as it's served cold. You could substitute the salmon for leftover tinned tuna and add any leftover peas or spinach along with the rest of the ingredients. You could also substitute the pasta for leftover rice or cous cous.

Method

Combine the mayonnaise and salmon. Add the salt and pepper and vegetables until everything is coated in mayo. Add to the pasta and stir to combine. Sprinkle with chopped parsley to serve, if desired.

Serves

1

Ingredients

½ tin salmon, drained and flaked, or 150 g leftover fresh salmon
1 tbsp mayonnaise
Salt and pepper
1 spring onion, diced
½ small red pepper, chopped (optional)
100 g leftover pasta
Handful of parsley, for serving if desired

LEFTOVER RICE SALAD WITH HAZELNUTS AND CRANBERRY DRESSING

Enjoy last night's rice with this delicious salad. A great way to use up any leftover cranberries.

Method

Reheat your rice in the microwave until piping hot. For each 80 g of rice, add 1–2 teaspoons of water and heat.

In a saucepan, fry the shallots, ginger and garlic until the shallots become translucent. Add the hazelnuts at the end to heat them through.

Add the rice and season with salt to taste.

For the dressing, place the dried cranberries in a cup of boiling water and let them stand and absorb the water for ten minutes. (If you're using frozen cranberries, follow the instructions on the packet as you may need to defrost them first or stand in the water for longer.)

Mix the cranberries with the remaining ingredients.

Pour the rice into a bowl along with the remaining ingredients. Pour the dressing on top and mix well.

Serves

1

Ingredients

80 g leftover rice
1 shallot, diced
½ cm ginger, finely chopped
1 clove garlic, minced
Handful of hazelnuts
Salt
Handful of parsley, roughly chopped
Handful of mint, roughly chopped
150 g kale
1 tbsp dried cranberries (frozen is fine too)
1 tbsp olive oil
1 tsp white wine vinegar
Salt and pepper to season

ARANCINI BALLS

Use up leftover rice or risotto with these delicious treats –
you can use up cheese or stuff diced vegetables into them,
such as any remaining spinach. Whizz up stale bread to
make the breadcrumbs for extra crunch.

Method

Heat the oil in a saucepan on a medium heat. Add the
onion, celery, garlic and a pinch of salt (and any extra
vegetables). Stir for five minutes. Remove from the heat,
then tip into a bowl with the rice and Parmesan. Mix the
ingredients together and add salt and pepper to taste.

Scoop out around 1 heaped tablespoon of the mixture
and add a 2-cm piece of mozzarella. Form a ball, then roll
in the flour. Shake off any excess flour, then roll in the
egg. Roll in the breadcrumbs until well coated. Repeat for
all six balls.

In a clean saucepan heat oil (enough to submerge the
balls) until tiny bubbles begin to form at the bottom and
a piece of bread sizzles immediately when dipped in.
Place the balls into the hot oil and fry until golden brown,
turning, if necessary, to cook evenly.

Serve sprinkled with chopped parsley, if desired.

Makes

6

Ingredients

1 tbsp olive oil
1 onion, finely diced
½ celery stick,
    finely diced
1 clove garlic, minced
Salt and pepper
250 g leftover rice
    or risotto
30 g Parmesan, grated
60 g mozzarella torn
    into six 2-cm pieces
30 g flour
1 egg, beaten
50 g breadcrumbs
Oil for deep frying
Handful of flat leaf
    parsley, chopped,
    to serve (optional)

STIR-FRIED RICE AND TUNA

A great way to use up any leftover rice you have. You can include tuna or salmon here for a light but delicious dinner that's full of health-boosting omega 3 fatty acids.

Method

Reheat rice in the microwave or in a saucepan over low heat until piping hot. Add some water to avoid the rice drying out.

Heat the oil in a wok over high heat.

Add the rice and garlic to the wok, stir-fry for one minute, then add the peas, tuna (or salmon), spring onions and soy sauce. Stir-fry quickly until heated through.

Take off the heat and stir in the pepper, tomatoes and olives.

Serve with extra soy sauce and spring onions.

Serves

1

Ingredients

80 g leftover cooked rice

1 tbsp olive oil

1 clove garlic, minced

60 g frozen peas

60 g can tuna (or salmon), drained

1 spring onion, finely sliced, plus extra to serve

1 tbsp light soy sauce, plus extra to serve

½ yellow pepper, diced

4 cherry tomatoes, halved

4 black olives, pitted

RICE-BOTTOMED QUICHE

This recipe is easily expandable, depending on how much rice you have remaining. You can either make individual servings in small ramekins or a larger quiche dish if you have more rice and veg to use up.

Method

Preheat the oven to 200°C. Grease an ovenproof ramekin with butter.

Beat the eggs in a medium-sized bowl and divide the mixture evenly into two separate bowls. Add the rice and olive oil to one bowl and mix.

Spread the rice over the bottom of the ramekin. Use the back of a spoon to press the mixture down so that it forms a smooth, firm base.

Sprinkle on some cheese and put the dish into the oven for 10 minutes.

Remove from the oven and add the vegetables and remaining cheese to the other egg mixture. Add the parsley and salt and pepper. Pour over the rice base and return to the oven for 25 minutes or until firm and golden Serve with toasted pine nuts if desired.

Makes

1 quiche

Ingredients

Butter for greasing
2 eggs
60 g leftover rice (enough to cover the base of the dish you are using)
1 tbsp olive oil
80 g grated cheese
125 g vegetables such as peppers or courgettes, sliced
Handful cherry tomatoes
Handful of parsley, chopped
Salt and pepper to taste
1 tbsp toasted pine nuts (optional)

MINI BREAD PUDDINGS

A warming pudding to enjoy after dinner at any time of the year. This is an easy way to use up stale or leftover bread. Serve with custard for extra sweetness.

Method

Preheat the oven to 180°C. Grease six ramekins or a six-hole muffin pan with 15 g of the butter.

In a bowl, whisk the milk, cream, sugar, cinnamon, nutmeg, vanilla and almond extract. Stir in the egg and egg yolk. Add the raisins and bread, and stir. Allow the mixture to soak into the bread for around five minutes.

Divide the mixture evenly between the muffin cups. You can sprinkle extra raisins or add some flaked almonds if you like. Bake for 20 minutes then remove from the oven.

In a saucepan, melt the remaining butter over a medium-low heat. Pour the butter and any nuts you may choose to use, such as roasted pecans or flaked almonds, over the puddings. Return to the oven for another 10 minutes.

Remove from the oven and cool slightly. Serve alone or with custard.

Serves

6

Ingredients

45 g unsalted butter
125 ml milk
125 g double cream
60 g granulated sugar
½ tsp cinnamon
Pinch of grated nutmeg
½ tsp vanilla extract
¼ tsp almond extract
1 egg, plus an extra yolk
125 g raisins, plus extra for topping
4–6 slices of bread, torn into small pieces
Flaked almonds and roasted pecans for topping (optional)

SPICY FRENCH TOAST

Use up stale bread for this tasty breakfast treat. Add some honey and berries for extra sweetness.

Method

Mix the warm milk, eggs and spices together.

Place the bread slices into a dish and cover with the mixture. Leave to soak for five minutes.

Heat a frying pan and add the butter. When the butter is melted and beginning to froth, add the bread slices and fry until golden, turning frequently.

Drizzle with honey and serve immediately.

Serves

2

Ingredients

2 eggs, beaten
150 ml milk, warmed
1 pinch ground
    cinnamon
1 pinch ground nutmeg
2 slices of stale bread,
    cut into fingers
25 g unsalted butter
Honey to serve
    (optional)

TOMATO AND CROUTON SALAD

A great summery dish which uses up your leftover bread and tomatoes. You could serve with yesterday's roast chicken or alongside roasted tofu or grilled fish.

Method

Heat some oil in a small saucepan, adding some salt and pepper. Add the bread and fry until golden brown. Set aside.

Place the tomatoes in a bowl and season with salt and pepper.

Rinse the capers, along with the onion and peppers.

Mix the ingredients together with your hands or a spatula.

Stir in the vinegar and olive oil.

Add salt and pepper to taste. Add more olive oil and vinegar if you desire.

Stir in the basil leaves, then serve.

Serves

1

Ingredients

50 g stale bread, torn into small pieces or sliced into 1-cm squares

4 cherry tomatoes, quartered

Salt and pepper

1 tbsp capers, drained

½ small red onion, peeled and very finely sliced

70 g red peppers from a jar, drained and chopped

¼ tsp red wine vinegar

1 tbsp olive oil

Fresh basil, to garnish

LEEK AND TOMATO BAKE

Ingredients

25 g butter, plus
   extra for greasing
1 large slice white
   bread, torn into
   chunks (you can use
   bread that's a little
   on the hard side)
½ leek, thinly sliced
1 garlic clove,
   finely chopped
25 g cherry tomatoes
1 egg
50 ml milk
25 g cheese, grated
Salt and pepper

This is an easy way to use up leftover white bread and any cheese pieces you may have, so it's a great recipe when you're having a fridge clear out.

Method

Heat oven to 200°C.

Grease a 10-cm dish or individual muffin cups and fill with the torn bread.

Place a medium pan on the heat and add the butter. When it starts to foam, add the leek and garlic, cooking over a medium heat for five minutes, stirring well.

Spoon softened leek mixture over the bread and top with cherry tomatoes.

In a mixing bowl, beat the egg, milk and grated cheese. Season, then pour over the bread.

Bake in the oven for 10–15 minutes, or until golden.

LEFTOVER MEAT

Each week most of us dig into some sort of meat dish – in fact, on average, those who live in the West eat around 90 kg of meat every year. If you're meal planning you could start the week with a roast, such as chicken, lamb, pork or beef, then use whatever is left for several meals throughout the week, or freeze for future use.

This section is your starting point for cooking tasty meals with your leftover meat. To find out how to store and freeze your meat or meat dishes, turn to page 18.

LEFTOVER LAMB AND RICE

A healthy and tasty way to use up your lamb (and any rice) leftovers. Best of all? It's a one-pot meal so there's very little washing up to do too.

Method

Pour the oil into a medium-sized pan, over a medium heat. Add the onion, turning the heat down to low, and give the onion a stir with a wooden spatula.

Add the garlic and spices. Stir for 2 minutes until the garlic, onion and spices are mixed and covered with the oil.

Add the stock and increase the heat to medium. Add the lamb and stir well to combine with the onion, garlic and spices. Bring to the boil, then cover the pan with a lid and lower the heat. Cook for 10 minutes, then remove the cinnamon stick. Remove the pan from the heat.

Reheat the rice in the microwave and add it to the pan along with the dried apricots, spring onion, tomato and herbs, stirring well. Add your seasoning as required. Serve, topped with herbs.

Serves

1

Ingredients

1 tbsp olive oil
½ large onion, finely chopped
1 garlic clove, finely chopped
¼ tsp turmeric
½ large cinnamon stick
½ lamb stock cube in 80 ml water
100 g cooked rice
125 g lamb leftovers, shredded or diced
50 g dried apricots
1 spring onion
1 large tomato, chopped
Small bunch parsley, chopped
Small bunch coriander, chopped
Salt and pepper

LEFTOVER ROAST CHICKEN SOUP

Chicken soup is good for the soul and those in a hurry. Simple to make, you can use whatever leftovers you have to hand, or bulk it up with leftover noodles, pasta, rice, lentils, or any additional veg, such as spinach, kale or mushrooms. Make up a batch from your leftover roast chicken and freeze for those cold winter days.

Method

Heat ½ tablespoon olive oil in a saucepan. Add the chopped onion and carrot. Cook on a low heat for 15 minutes. Pour in the chicken stock, bringing it to the boil. Cover with the pan lid, then simmer for 10 minutes.

Add the shredded leftover roast chicken and the vegetables you're using and season to taste. Add the pasta, rice, noodles or lentils if using.

Simmer for five minutes, or until heated through. Serve with bread if desired.

Serves

1

Ingredients

½ tbsp olive oil

1 onion, chopped

1 medium carrot, chopped

250 ml chicken stock

100 g leftover roast chicken, shredded and skin removed (see p.41 for how to use up leftover chicken skin)

400 g vegetables you want to use up, such as broccoli, cauliflower, leeks, courgette, frozen peas, spinach etc

125 g leftover pasta, rice, noodles or lentils (if using)

LEFTOVER CHICKEN AND MUSHROOM RISOTTO

A simple mid-week recipe that uses up leftover roast chicken and any bits of veg, such as spinach, kale or peppers, you may have lurking in your crisper.

Method

Heat the butter in a saucepan over a low heat, being careful not to brown or burn it. Add the onion and stir until it is coated in the butter. Allow to cook for five minutes until soft.

Add the thyme sprig and mushrooms, stirring to coat the ingredients with the butter. If you're using other veg, add this now. Cook for five minutes, then add the rice and stir.

Pour in a ladleful of the stock and stir to combine all the ingredients. When the rice has soaked up the liquid, add another ladleful, and keep stirring. Continue in this way until all of the liquid has been used and absorbed. Taste the rice and add more water and continue cooking if it needs further softening. Add the chicken pieces and Parmesan and stir well until heated through properly. Season with salt and pepper and serve, adding chopped parsley on top if desired.

Serves

2

Ingredients

30 g unsalted butter
1 onion, finely chopped
1 sprig fresh thyme
Handful of mushrooms, sliced
200 g Arborio risotto rice
500 ml chicken stock
200 g leftover roast chicken, shredded
40 g Parmesan cheese
Salt and pepper
Chopped parsley, to serve (optional)

LEFTOVER ROAST CHICKEN PAD THAI

Put your leftover roast chicken to good use, with this healthy Thai meal.

Method

First, prepare the coriander. Chop the stalks separately and put the leaves aside for topping. Prepare the noodles according to the packet instructions.

While the noodles are cooking, heat a wok until lightly smoking. Add the oil.

Add the garlic, coriander stalks, carrot, shallot and mangetout, stirring for ten seconds. Add the pad Thai paste and stir until combined.

Make a well in the centre, add the egg and fry for one minute until the egg is cooked. Add the drained noodles and chicken. Stir to combine and heat the chicken through.

Serve, adding coriander leaves, raw beansprouts and peanuts as required. Squeeze some lime juice over the dish before serving.

Serves

1

Ingredients

80 g dried rice noodles
20 ml oil
120 g roast chicken, shredded or sliced
1 garlic clove, chopped finely
Handful of coriander
1 carrot, peeled and cut into small slices (matchstick sized)
1 shallot, cut into 3-cm lengths
40 g mangetout, trimmed and halved
80 g jar pad Thai paste
1 egg, lightly whisked
25 g beansprouts
1 tbsp roasted unsalted peanuts
Lime juice, to serve

COLD ROAST BEEF WITH ROASTED TOMATOES AND FETA CHEESE

Use up leftover roast beef with this tasty salad, perfect for lunches or an easy dinner.

Method

Preheat the oven to 180°C. Place the tomatoes into an ovenproof dish alongside the garlic. Drizzle over the olive oil, and sprinkle with salt and pepper. Place into the oven for 10 minutes.

Meanwhile, make the dressing. Whisk all the ingredients together in a mixing bowl and pour into a dressing container. Add salt and pepper and mix well.

Remove the tomatoes from the oven and allow to cool a little.

Place the salad leaves on the plate, then add the beef, feta, shallot and roasted tomatoes. Pour on the dressing.

Serves

1

Ingredients

Handful of tomatoes
1 garlic clove, sliced
1 tsp olive oil
Salt and pepper
Handful of salad leaves
150 g thin slices cold
    leftover roast beef
80 g feta, cubed
1 shallot, finely
    chopped

For the dressing:
2 tbsp olive oil
Juice of half a lemon
1 tsp horseradish
    or mustard
1 tsp honey
Salt and pepper

LEFTOVER ROAST BEEF AND VEG HOTPOT

This dish is ideal to enjoy on a cold winter's evening.

Method

Preheat the oven to 180°C. Then heat 1 tbsp oil in a pan. Add the vegetables (if not already cooked). Season, and stir. Add the bay leaf and cook for 10–15 minutes. If you are using leftover vegetables in this dish, just give them a quick refresh: use less oil and seasoning. Just two minutes on the stove will give them some life and added flavour.

Add the leftover cooked beef to the pan and stir in the flour, allspice and tomato purée. Add the red wine, if using, and the beef stock, passata and Worcestershire sauce. Simmer for 45 minutes.

Remove the bay leaf. Pour the beef mixture into a small ovenproof dish. Once the mixture has settled, layer the potato slices on top, overlapping the edges slightly. Brush the potatoes with the remaining 1 tbsp oil and cover the dish with a lid or foil. Bake in the oven for 30 minutes or until the potato is golden. If you're using pre-cooked potatoes this will need less time. Remove the lid for the last 10 minutes to allow the topping to turn crisp and golden.

Serves

1

Ingredients

2 tbsp olive oil

1 bay leaf

1 onion, sliced

½ leek, thickly sliced

1 carrot, chopped (if not using leftovers)

1 parsnip, chopped (if not using leftovers)

Salt and pepper

125 g leftover roast beef, chopped

1 tsp plain flour

¼ tsp allspice

1 tbsp tomato purée

25 ml red wine (optional)

125 ml beef stock

85 ml passata

Splash of Worcestershire sauce

125 g desiree or sweet potatoes, finely sliced

TASTY TURKEY SALAD

If you've enjoyed a turkey roast, this salad will give your digestive system a welcome break, while using up the remainder of the bird.

Method

Arrange the salad leaves onto a plate. Add the turkey slices to the lettuce leaves. Add the tomatoes on top. Season to taste and sprinkle a little parsley on top if desired.

Mix together the dressing ingredients in a small jug and drizzle over the salad before serving.

Serves

1

Ingredients

Generous handfuls
   of salad leaves
Handful of sliced
   leftover turkey
3 tomatoes, halved
Parsley (optional)
Salt and pepper
   to season

For the dressing:
¼ red onion,
   finely chopped
1 tsp red wine vinegar
1 tsp honey
Spoonful low-fat
   yoghurt

LEFTOVER TURKEY, CHEESE AND TOMATO BAKE

Another great way to use up turkey leftovers, although you could just as easily replace turkey with any remaining chicken or lamb you may have. Add breadcrumbs, or make some easily with leftover bread, and sprinkle on top for extra crunch.

Method

Preheat the oven to 220°C.

Add the oil to a saucepan, then fry the onion and garlic until soft. Add the tomatoes, oregano, sugar, vinegar and season with salt and pepper if you like. Stir until it becomes a thick sauce, then add the turkey.

Transfer to a small baking dish. Tear the mozzarella into small pieces and scatter on top of the mixture. Season with salt and pepper. Place in the oven and bake for 20 minutes or until the breadcrumbs are golden. Serve with a salad or mashed potatoes if you have some to use up.

Serves

2

Ingredients

1 tbsp olive oil
1 onion, chopped
2 garlic cloves, crushed
2 tsp dried oregano
200 g chopped tomatoes
2 tsp sugar
2 tsp vinegar
Salt and pepper to season
240 g leftover turkey (or whichever leftover meat you are using)
1 ball mozzarella

3 tacos

300 g roast pork
    leftovers, shredded
Mexican spices
    (optional)
Salt and pepper
Pinch of chilli flakes
    (optional)
60 g shredded cabbage
1 avocado, diced
½ carrot, grated
50 g grated cheese
3 taco shells
60 g sour cream
    (optional)
1 avocado, mashed
    (optional)
Juice of ½ lime

LEFTOVER PORK TACOS

Turn your leftover roast pork into these delicious taco Tuesday treats. Best of all, you can use straggly bits of veg from your fridge for some varied toppings. If you don't have taco shells you can use a wrap. Just spray it with olive oil and place in the oven for around five minutes. It'll become crispy and ideal as a taco substitute.

Method

Preheat the oven to 180°C.

Heat the pork in the microwave for two minutes. Check that all pieces are piping hot. If you like your tacos spicy, heat the pork in a pan with a little olive oil, then add a sprinkle of Mexican spice, or simply season with salt, pepper and some chilli flakes.

Heat the taco shells for around 3–5 minutes in the oven. Place on a board or large plate.

Arrange the shredded pork, cabbage, avocado, grated carrot and cheese into separate bowls.

Combine the sour cream and mashed avocado in a separate bowl. Pile the food into your tacos. Top with the avocado dressing and a squeeze of lime.

LEFTOVER VEGETABLES

If you always end up with leftover vegetables, don't throw them away. There's a huge number of ways you can use up these healthy ingredients, including soups, sauces and sneaky recipes so that your kids, or any fussy adults, will finally eat that broccoli!

LEFTOVER VEG PIES

If you've got some roast veg remaining use them up in this delicious pie recipe. You can freeze them after cooking and pop them in your lunchbox to be warmed up for a tasty lunchtime treat.

Method

Preheat the oven to 200°C. Place a saucepan on a medium heat and add the olive oil.

Sauté the onion and garlic until soft. Add the flour and chicken stock, stirring until combined. Bring to the boil then simmer until the sauce has thickened.

Add the vegetables. If some need to be cooked, add these first and simmer for around 15 minutes, then add the leftovers. Cook until the liquid reduces and set aside.

Grease and line a 20-cm pie tin, or a muffin tray with shortcrust pastry. Cut the pieces larger than the base in order to create the sides of the pie.

Fill the pastry case with the vegetable mixture and brush the edge of the pastry with some egg. Cover the tops of the pie, or pies, with pastry and press the edges firmly to seal. Brush the top with egg and make slits to allow steam to escape. Bake for 20 minutes or until golden.

Makes

1 large pie or 6 small individual pies

Ingredients

1 tbsp olive oil
1 small onion, chopped
1 garlic clove, crushed
375 g plain flour
375 ml vegetable stock
750 g leftover/ fresh veg
Butter, for greasing
2 sheets shortcrust pastry or enough shortcrust pastry sheets to create the base and top of your pie(s)
1 egg, beaten

PUMPKIN SOUP

A simple way to use up leftover roast pumpkin. Enjoy with crusty bread or freeze so you can reheat it on a cold winter's day for a simple lunch.

Method

Place a large saucepan on a medium heat and add the olive oil and butter.

When the butter has melted, add the onion and garlic. Add the curry powder or paste and cook for two minutes, stirring continuously.

Pour in the vegetable stock and bring to the boil. Add the pumpkin to the stock and simmer for five minutes.

Add the mixture to a food processor or use a hand blender and liquidize.

Quickly roast some pumpkin seeds by adding a handful to a small pan with one teaspoon of oil. Roast for around two minutes or until they begin to brown. Remove from the heat and transfer to a small bowl.

Serve the soup with crème fraiche, balsamic vinegar and pumpkin seeds. Add pepper to taste.

Serves

2

Ingredients

1 tbsp olive oil, plus a little extra
15 g unsalted butter
1 large onion, finely chopped
1 clove garlic, peeled and finely chopped
1 tsp curry powder or paste
500 ml vegetable stock
500 g leftover roast pumpkin, roughly chopped
Pumpkin seeds, for garnish
2 tbsp crème fraiche, to serve
1 tbsp balsamic vinegar, to serve
Pepper, to serve

WHITE BEAN AND MUSHROOM SOUP

(Ve)

If you're feeling a little run down, kidney beans can help give your immune system a boost. Add in some leftover mushrooms – you can use porcini, shiitake, brown or white – plus veg such as carrots: anything you have and want to use up.

Method

Preheat the oven to 180°C.

If the mushrooms haven't been cooked, roast them in the oven by lying them flat on a baking tray on parchment paper. Drizzle with half the oil and sprinkle with salt. Roast for five minutes. Then remove and set aside.

Meanwhile, add the rest of the oil to a saucepan and add the onion and garlic and cook until slightly caramelized.

Pour in the stock, beans, carrots and any leftover veg. Bring to the boil and simmer for around 20 minutes, stirring occasionally. Add the roasted mushrooms, stirring them through the soup.

Serve with crusty bread if desired.

Serves

1

Ingredients

100 g mushrooms, chopped
1 tbsp olive oil
Salt and pepper
1 small onion, chopped
1 garlic clove, chopped
250 g vegetable stock (or use water)
½ can white beans (or use kidney beans – whichever you have in the cupboard or left over)
1 carrot, chopped (or other leftover veg)
Selection of herbs such as thyme or sage

VEGGIE NOODLE SOUP

This warming noodle soup is like a hug in food form. Not only is it simple to make, but you can add in pretty much any vegetables you like!

Method

Put the garlic, soy sauce, rice wine, sesame oil and vegetable stock into a pan. Bring to the boil, then simmer for 10 minutes with the lid on.

Meanwhile, cook the noodles according to the packet instructions. Drain and set to one side.

If you are using vegetables that aren't already cooked, put the vegetable oil in a wok or pan over a high heat, add your uncooked vegetables and stir-fry for 2–3 minutes.

Put the leafy greens into the vegetable stock 2 minutes before you serve.

To serve, put the cooked noodles into a bowl, add the stir-fried vegetables on top, then pour over the broth and leafy greens. Add chilli oil, chilli flakes or spring onions if desired.

Makes

1

Ingredients

2 cloves garlic, peeled and crushed

1 tsp soy sauce

1 tbsp rice wine

1 tbsp sesame oil

500 ml vegetable stock

80 g dried rice noodles

Leftover vegetables, sliced thinly (such as carrots, courgettes or mushrooms)

1 tbsp vegetable oil (optional)

Handful of leafy greens, such as cabbage or bok choy

Chilli oil or chilli flakes (optional)

Spring onions, chopped (optional)

CAULIFLOWER AND BROCCOLI PASTA BAKE

Serve with a side salad for extra goodness.

Method

Put the pasta on to boil in salted water following the packet instructions. Remove from the heat and drain just before it's al dente.

Preheat the oven to 180°C. Melt the butter in a medium-sized saucepan, then stir in the flour until it forms a paste.

Remove the pan from the heat. Gradually add the milk, stirring continuously. Add the broccoli and simmer for 20 minutes, or until the florets begin to break up. Add the grated cheese, continuing to stir to keep the sauce smooth. Add salt and pepper to taste.

In a small baking dish, pour in the pasta to cover the bottom of dish. Then arrange the cauliflower over the top.

Pour the sauce over the pasta and cauliflower. Add the breadcrumbs and some more grated cheese. Season it again, and sprinkle with the chopped thyme leaves.

Cook for 25–30 minutes or until the top is golden and crunchy.

Serves

1

Ingredients

Handful of broccoli florets, cut into small pieces

Handful of cauliflower florets, cut into small pieces

60 g breadcrumbs

1 sprig fresh thyme, leaves removed and chopped

80 g uncooked pasta

1 clove garlic, peeled and finely sliced

15 g unsalted butter

15 g plain flour

120 ml milk

25 g cheese, grated (plus extra for the topping)

BULGUR WHEAT, SPINACH AND AUBERGINE PILAF

(Ve)

A tasty nutty lunch or dinnertime meal to use up your spinach and aubergine. You can serve this on its own for a delicious vegan meal, or you can add lamb if you prefer.

Method

Preheat the oven to 180°C.

Cook the bulgur wheat as per packet instructions.

While this is cooking, place the aubergine on a baking tray lined with baking paper. Brush both sides of the aubergine with olive oil and put into the oven until browned.

When the bulgar is cooked, combine with the spinach, aubergine and onion.

For the dressing:

Mix the oil, lemon/lime juice and zest, chillies, cumin, salt and pepper in a bowl and stir well.

Pour the dressing over the bulgur and veg, seasoning to taste. Serve with a wedge of lemon or lime and sprinkle the zest on top.

Serves

1

Ingredients

100 g bulgur wheat
½ aubergine sliced into rounds then sliced into triangular shapes
2 tbsp olive oil
Handful of spinach, roughly chopped
½ red onion, finely chopped

For the dressing:

1 tbsp olive oil
½ tbsp lemon or lime juice, plus zest
¼ tsp crushed chillies
¼ tsp ground cumin
Salt and pepper

LEFTOVER VEG SPIRAL TART (V)

Method

Preheat the oven to 200°C. Grease a pastry dish or tart tin (around 22 cm or suitable to the amount of vegetables you have).

Heat 1 tablespoon of oil in a large frying pan. Cook the onion until it begins to soften, then add the garlic and cook for another minute. Add the butternut squash or pumpkin and sage along with a tablespoon of water. Cover and cook for 10–12 minutes until soft. Remove from the heat and mash until smooth.

Add the vegetable strips to a bowl with 2 tablespoons of oil, the agave syrup and the chilli flakes then mix.

Place the pastry into the pie dish and trim the edges. Spread the mash evenly over the bottom. Make a "rose" by taking three vegetable strips and rolling until you've made a tight spiral. Place in the centre of the tart.

Place the remaining ribbons around the rose, creating a concentric circle. Brush the remaining olive oil over the tart once you've finished. Place in the oven and bake for 40–45 minutes.

Makes

1 tart

Ingredients

Butter, for greasing
5 tbsp olive oil
1 small onion, finely diced
2 cloves garlic, crushed
250 g butternut squash or pumpkin, cubed in 1-cm pieces
4 sage leaves
3 courgettes, finely sliced
3 carrots, finely sliced
3 aubergines, finely sliced
1 tbsp agave syrup
1 tsp chilli flakes
1 sheet shortcrust pastry that's slightly larger than the tart tin

LENTIL BOLOGNESE

Use that tin of lentils from the back of the cupboard for this delicious dish which can be kept in the freezer for busy weeknights.

Method

Heat the oil in a large frying pan over medium heat. Add the onion, celery, carrot and garlic and cook for five minutes or until all the ingredients have softened. Stir in the passata, tomatoes, kale and spinach (if using). Add the water, bringing to the boil. Add the lentils and thyme and season to taste. Cook for 15 minutes or until the sauce has thickened slightly.

Meanwhile, cook the pasta according to the packet instructions. When ready, drain. Ladle the pasta into bowls and add the lentil Bolognese on top.

> ## TIP
>
> If you like the meat version of Bolognese, you can use a combination of both mince and lentils or use lentils to pad out your recipe if you only have a small amount of mince in your freezer.

Serves

4

Ingredients

2 tsp olive oil
1 onion, diced
2 stalks celery, finely chopped
1 carrot, grated
1–2 garlic cloves, minced
700 ml passata
2 tomatoes, seeded and diced
400 g can lentils, drained and rinsed (or use leftovers)
Handful of spinach (optional)
Handful of kale (optional)
125 ml water
2 tsp dried thyme
300 g dried pasta

4 fritters

500 g leftover
vegetables,
cut into cubes
2 potatoes, raw
and grated
1 onion, finely chopped
3 eggs, separated
2 tbsp olive oil
125 g self raising flour
Salt and pepper

FRITTERS WITH V LEFTOVER VEGETABLES

Put those leftover veg to good use with these tasty fritters. Add potato or sweet potato mash to make extra or add some rice or quinoa. These are also great for freezing.

Method

Place the vegetables and potato into a bowl and combine.

Add the egg yolks and combine until all the ingredients are coated in yolk.

Beat the egg whites until foamy, then add to the vegetable mixture.

In a bowl, add the flour and salt and pepper.

Form balls with the egg and vegetable mixture, and roll in the flour until fully coated.

Heat a medium-sized saucepan and add the oil.

Place the balls into the saucepan, flattening them into a patty shape.

Cook until golden brown on both sides. Serve with mayonnaise, green salad and a squeeze of lemon.

LEFTOVER FRUIT

Sometimes we start the week with the best of intentions, only to be faced on Friday with a bowl of fruit that's quickly going off. While fruit does lose some of its nutrients as it ages, there's still loads of ways to enjoy the goodness in smoothies, compotes, cakes or puddings.

GOOD MORNING SMOOTHIES (v)

If your fruit has gone a little soft you can still use it in a smoothie. Add some coconut water or your preferred plant-based milk as your blend. Add ice for an especially cool treat.

Method

Place all the ingredients into a blender and blend until completely mixed.

Add some ice, if desired, and blend again.

Pour into a glass and enjoy.

Serves

1

Ingredients

Handful of leftover fruit: banana, strawberries, blueberries, or a combination of them all
1 tsp honey
200 ml coconut water or plant-based milk
Ice (optional)

FRUIT PULP MUFFINS

If you've enjoyed a fresh juice for breakfast you'll be left with a lot of pulp in your juicer. Put it to use with these delicious muffins that can be served warm alongside yoghurt topped with lemon zest.

Method

Preheat the oven to 200°C. Line a muffin pan with paper cases.

In a bowl combine the flour, sugar, salt and baking powder.

In a separate bowl combine the oil, egg and milk. Whisk together then pour the liquid over the dry ingredients.

Add the pulp and any extra fruit, such as blueberries or strawberries. Stir to combine the ingredients evenly.

Pour the mixture into the individual muffin cases.

Bake for 25 minutes or until cooked through.

Makes

9–12

Ingredients

375 g plain flour
190 g caster sugar
Pinch of salt
2 tsp baking powder
80 ml vegetable oil
1 egg
80 ml milk
150 g fruit pulp

NECTARINE SALAD

Serve this healthy and delicious salad alongside a roasted sweet potato or fish dinner. Or add some roasted nuts for protein and enjoy on its own.

Method

Make the dressing first. In a bowl, stir the honey, balsamic vinegar and shallot. Whisk together and add the olive oil. Add salt and pepper to taste.

In a small pan, toast the almonds until brown.

On a plate, arrange the rest of the salad ingredients.

Add the dressing and top with black pepper and the toasted almonds.

Serves

1

Ingredients

For the dressing:
1 tsp clear honey
½ tbsp balsamic vinegar
1 shallot, finely chopped
40 ml olive oil
Salt and pepper

For the salad:
15 g flaked almonds
1 ripe nectarine, sliced
Handful of watercress
Handful of salad leaves
1 large tomato, roughly chopped
Handful of cucumber pieces

PLUM, QUINOA AND OAT CRUMBLE

(V)

If you're gluten intolerant this warming dessert is just for you. Simple to prepare, this is an easy recipe to whip up if you fancy a sweet treat.

Method

Preheat the oven to 180°C. Grease an ovenproof dish, such as a ramekin, with butter.

Using a food processor, place the oats, quinoa flour and sugar into the bowl. Blend well to combine.

Add the cubed butter and pulse, until the mixture resembles breadcrumbs.

Meanwhile, mix together the lemon juice and caster sugar. Pour into the ovenproof dish.

Place the plums in the dish and spread the crumble topping on top. Place in the oven for 25 minutes, until the fruit is bubbling and the crumble topping is golden brown.

Serves

1

Ingredients

For the crumble:
40 g gluten-free oats
60 g quinoa, ground in a spice grinder or blender to make flour
10 g muscovado sugar
25 g chilled butter, cut into cubes, plus extra for greasing

For the filling:
Juice of ½ lemon
65 g caster sugar
250 g plums, halved and pitted

APRICOT AND ALMOND TART

V

Even if your fruit is a little past its best-by date you can bake with it for some extra sweet treats.

Method

Preheat the oven to 180°C.

Place the apricot halves, cut-side up, in an ovenproof dish. Drizzle the apricots with the orange juice and ½ tablespoon of the honey. Roast for 30 minutes, basting halfway through with the juice, until the apricots are soft.

Grease a shallow 20-cm pie or tart case and line with shortcrust pastry, covering the base and sides. Bake for 20–25 minutes until crisp and golden. Remove and leave to cool completely.

Mix the yoghurt with the remaining honey and half the orange zest. Spoon into the tart case, then add the baked apricots on top, along with any juices.

Top with the almonds, remaining orange zest and a drizzle more honey if you like and put in the oven for a further 5 minutes so the apricots are warm and the almonds slightly toasted. Serve immediately.

Serves

6–8

Ingredients

7 ripe apricots, halved and pitted

125 ml orange juice or the juice of an orange

3 tbsp honey, plus extra for drizzling

1 sheet shortcrust pastry

500 g Greek yoghurt

Zest of an orange

10 g flaked almonds

CHERRY DELIGHT ICE CREAM

Make your own delicious ice cream using leftover cherries. A perfect way to cool down in summer.

Method

Place the pitted cherries into a saucepan.

Add the caster sugar.

Stir over a medium heat until the sugar is completely dissolved. The cherries should be nice and soft.

Remove from the heat and allow the mixture to cool.

Pour the mixture into a food processor or blender and pulse until the cherries are roughly chopped.

In a bowl, pour the cream and beat, using an electric beater or whisk, until soft peaks are formed.

Add the cream cheese and condensed milk and beat until smooth.

Stir the cherry mixture through the cream. Pour into a loaf tin or airtight container and freeze overnight.

Serves

8

Ingredients

700 g cherries, pitted
125 g caster sugar
600 ml whipping cream
250 g cream cheese
395 ml can sweetened condensed milk

LEFTOVER VEG AND ORANGE CAKE

This is a wonderful way to use up leftover fruit AND veg. And what could be better than cake? Serve alongside yoghurt or ice cream if desired.

Method

Preheat the oven to 180°C. Grease and line a deep 20-cm cake tin with baking paper.

Mix the sultanas with the zest and juice from the oranges. Place in the microwave on high for two minutes.

Combine the flour, brown sugar, spices, bicarbonate of soda and pinch of salt in a large bowl.

Mix the eggs with the melted butter and sultana mixture, then add to the dry ingredients. Stir until combined.

Add the grated veg, stirring well. When combined, scoop the mixture into the baking tin, spreading evenly.

Bake for 35–40 mins, or until a skewer poked in the centre comes out clean. Allow the cake to cool in the tin.

Before serving sift the icing sugar over the cake and top with some almonds, if desired.

Makes

1 cake

Ingredients

140 g sultanas or raisins
Zest and juice of 2 oranges
300 g self raising flour
300 g light brown sugar
2 tsp mixed spice
1 tsp ground ginger
1 tsp bicarbonate of soda
Salt
4 large eggs, beaten
200 g butter, melted, plus extra for greasing
300 g carrots, parsnips, pumpkin, butternut squash or swede, grated
Icing sugar for dusting
Handful of almonds (optional)

Ingredients

100 g broccoli florets
100 g kale
1 apple, peeled and
    cored (you can
    keep the skin
    on if you like)
2 sticks celery (chop
    into smaller pieces
    before juicing –
    around 4 cm long)

GREEN IS GOOD

This super-green juice requires a juicer – if you only have a blender you may need to sieve the liquid to remove the pulp, although taste it first to see whether you like pulp in your juice.

Method

Juice all the ingredients and serve. You can dilute the mixture with coconut water or water if it's too thick.

OTHER LEFTOVERS

If you find yourself with some leftover birthday cake, don't let it go to waste. In this chapter, you'll find a simple but delicious way to enjoy sponge after the celebrations have died down. And don't be too quick to throw away dairy products that are approaching their use-by date, because there are ways to turn them into delicious treats.

CHOCOLATE SPONGE TRUFFLES

A delicious way to use up leftover cake. You could use coconut sprinkles or chocolate chips for different versions.

Method

Using a food processor, blitz the sponge into fine crumbs.

Add the cream cheese and combine to form a dough-like mixture.

Roll the mixture into golf ball sized portions.

Place onto a baking tray and freeze for 30 minutes.

Meanwhile, melt the white chocolate chips in a heatproof bowl over a saucepan of simmering water. When the balls have frozen, dip each one into the white chocolate.

Roll in the sprinkles (optional) and place onto the baking tray to set.

They will keep in the fridge for five days or in the freezer for three months.

Makes

10–12

Ingredients

320 g leftover chocolate cake (vanilla sponge cake will also work)

160 g cream cheese

200 g white chocolate chips

200 g coconut sprinkles (optional)

CHEESY TOAST

Make the most of leftover cheese and milk that's near its use-by date with this deliciously easy dish.

Method

Preheat the grill. Place the bread under the grill and brown on one side. Remove from the grill.

In a bowl, mix together the cheese, milk and spring onion. Spread over the toasted side of one piece of bread.

Place the other slice of bread on top, untoasted side up. Return to the grill and brown until the cheese bubbles.

Serves

1

Ingredients

2 slices bread
125 g cheese
1 tbsp milk
1 spring onion,
    finely chopped

VANILLA MILK PUDDING (v)

Leftover milk makes a sweet and decadent pudding for you to enjoy. Add pistachios, flaked almonds or berries if you have them.

Method

In a bowl, mix together 60 ml of milk and the rice flour to make a paste.

In a saucepan, bring the rest of the milk and sugar to the boil.

Remove from the heat and stir in the paste. Add the remaining ingredients.

Return the saucepan to the heat and stir until the mixture boils and thickens. Cook for another two minutes, continuing to stir.

Pour into two separate bowls. Cover with wrap and place in the fridge for up to two hours.

Serve with chopped nuts, a drizzle of honey and some sprigs of mint if you wish.

Serves

2

Ingredients

125 ml milk
125 g rice flour
2 tbsp caster sugar
½ tsp vanilla essence
¼ tsp cinnamon
¼ tsp cardamom
Honey, for serving (optional)
Nuts, for serving (optional)
Mint, for serving (optional)

FROZEN YOGHURT FRUIT TREATS

Use up leftover yoghurt and berries with these cooling summery treats.

Method

Blend the yoghurt and berries until smooth.

Pour into ice lolly moulds, insert wooden lolly sticks, and freeze overnight.

If you don't have ice lolly moulds you can pour the mixture onto a baking tray, lined with baking paper. Place in a freezer and break off pieces to enjoy whenever you want a cold treat.

Makes

6 lollies

Ingredients

250 g yoghurt
125 g berries, blended

CONCLUSION

There are so many ways to use up leftovers and hopefully you've been inspired to begin a new way of shopping and cooking. Remember, it takes a while to form new habits, so be kind to yourself and take small steps along your new journey of a waste-free life.

Being organized with your food purchases and menu planning is good for your bank balance but also your stress levels. Knowing what you have available to cook takes the wonder and angst out of dinner planning; being creative with leftovers means that you'll be introducing new flavours and ingredients to your repertoire – who knows, you may find a new family favourite.

An important point to remember: don't try to change everything at once. However, if every week, then every day, you can make one small change, or stop yourself from throwing away leftover food, then you're contributing to big changes in the world.

And that's definitely something to celebrate.

Have you enjoyed this book?
If so, find us on Facebook at *Summersdale Publishers*, on Twitter at @summersdale
and on Instagram at @summersdalebooks and
get in touch. We'd love to hear from you!

www.summersdale.com

Image credits